This Is How I Spoke To The World.

The Voice Within Me.

Nancy Singh

BookLeaf Publishing

India | USA | UK

Made with ❤ on the BookLeaf Publishing Platform
www.bookleafpub.in
www.bookleafpub.com

Dedication

Dear Readers,

This collection was born out of quiet nights unexpected
thoughts, and emotions that
refused to be silenced. Each poem is a reflection of
something deeply felt- sometimes fleeting, sometimes
overwhelming,
but always real.

If you've never felt these emotions before, I hope life
continues to be kind to you.
But if you have- know this you're not alone.
You never were.

These words are my way of reaching out- a reminder
that even in your most vulnerable moments someone,
somewhere, understands.

With all my warts,
Nancy Singh.

Preface

This is How I spoke to the world is not just a collection
of poem-
it is a collection of moments I lived emotions I could no
longer contains, and silence I refused to carry any longer.

Each word in these pages comes from a place that once
hurt, once healed, once bloomed quietly in the corner of
my soul.
Sometimes whispered, sometimes cried, these poem are
my way of telling the world: "*I felt this. I survived.*"

I never knew how to say things aloud, so I said them in
verses.
This is How spoke to the world- with trembling honesty,
with scattered metaphors, and with the feel less alone
while reading them.

To those who've felt too much or not enough, to those
who've loved deeply, broken silently,
or found strength in their softest parts-
this book is for you.
Let this be a conversation between you and me.
One where no voice is too quiet, and no feeling is too
much.

Acknowledgements

I am deeply grateful to the team at Book Leaf
Publication for believing in my voice and
helping me bring *This is How I spoke to the World* to
life.

To everyone who walked beside me-
and even those who walked away- thank you.
Your presence, your lesson, and your absences have all
shaped these words.

This book is for every soul who has stayed,
every soul who has left , and every soul who is yet to
come.
Thank you for being a part of my story.

With love and gratitude,
Nancy Singh.

1. The Child I Was.

I was an extroverted child,
with truth resting easy on my tongue,
smiles blooming like spring
without a second thought.

Innocence danced in my words,
I knew not how to fake a laugh
or forge a friend.
Joy was my natural rhythm, and laughter my lullaby.

But my honesty,
too raw for polished hearts,
caused discomfort in those,
I held dearest.

Their glance cooled,
their words grew sharp-
I was scolded
for saying what others swallowed.
Told to hush, to mold.

to be anything but bold.

Guilt crept in like a shadow,
fear followed close behind.
And slowly ,
the child who spoke with stars in
her eyes learned silence.

The extrovert faded,
step by step,
until she stood at the edge
of her voice,
an introvert-
still smiling,
but quieter now.

2. I am a Paradox.

I am a paradox, a living disguise,
smiling in sunlight while bracing
for cries.

I feel the world with heart open wide,
Then drift into silence, with nothing inside,
At times I bloom with a self-loving grace,
Then scorn my reflection, lost in
the haze.

A tangle of truth in a single
souls calls-
I am everything....
and sometimes nothing at all.

I am a paradox, tender yet taut,
A symphony playing a single,
strange thought.

3. Gave it all for nothing.

It shatters the hearts, a million ways,
when you gave your all through countless days.

Dreams laid down at love's command,
Hopes buried deep like a grains of sand.

You sacrificed, you stood so tall,
Only to hear, "You did nothing at all."
or worse- " Did I ever ask you to ?"
As if your soul had not broken into.

4. Too Human

You feel so deeply,
it blurs the lines-
Are you an overthinker,
too sensitive,
emotional,
or just.....
too human
for the world that worships
logic and label feelings as flaws?

5. Gamophobic Heart

I am a gamophobic,
A wanderer in loves chaotic maze-
Sometimes I crave a hand to hold,
A soul to warm my colder days.

I watch the world in pairs and ties,
frustrated glances, silent cries,
and in those moments, I feel free,
Grateful for the solitude in me.

Yet deep inside, a whisper stirs,
of butterflies and loving words-
The thrill of someone knowing me,
Like secret poems and gentle tea,

But love,
I know, is double-edged-
The same sweet hand can leave you wrecked.
The trauma that a heart can bear,
Makes me hold my own with care.

So, here I stand, alone yet whole,
Treating myself like I'm the goal-
For if loves comes, it must be true.
Not just a spark, but fire that grew.

6. Race

I've seen lovers turns fighters,
their words- no longer bridges, but blades.

Each one racing
to be the rudest,
to land the harshest blow,
as if cruelty could crown a winner
in a war of hearts.

But no one wins
when silence screams louder than love,
and every sharp words
craves away
what once held them close.

They don't see it-
in trying to win the fight,
they're losing the bond.

7. What Do I Tell the Child Within?

Sometimes,
parents forget
how words- just words-
can leave wounds no time can truly heal.

A sharp look,
a careless phrase,
a cruel comparison dressed as concern-
they settle like thorns in a child's heart.

"Why can't you be more like them?"
"Is this all you could do?"
Echoes that return
every result day,
long after the marks have faded.

Now, as an adult,
I've learned to understand-
that parents are not perfect.

They, too, carry their own brokenness.

But how do I explain that
to the child I once was?
The one still curled up inside me,
craving an apology that never came.

How do I teach her to heal
from wounds no one else remembers,
when even love came
wrapped in silence?

8. I heard about you from others.

It feels worse than a breakup-
Losing the friend you once planned your life with.
The one who swore to stay in touch,
But now, silence is all they send.

You called.
They were "busy".
You waited.
And waited....
Now it's been more than a year.

A dear friend turned into a stranger,
An acquaintance in passing conversation.
The same soul who once shared
Every small detail of their day.
Now appears only through stories
Told by others.

It stings.

So much, you start to question-
Was I ever truly a friend ?
Or just a phase in their life?
A chapter they've closed.
While I still reread the lines.
Trying to find where I went wrong.

9. The Unspoken Call.

Sometimes I just want to call,
Pour out my soul, confess it all-
The weight I carry, silent and deep,
The thoughts that haunts me when I sleep.

Nothing's happened, yet here I stand,
with aching heart and trembling hands.
A storm inside, no cause, no name,
Just shadows dancing in quiet shame.

I long to speak, to just be heard,
To find some comfort in a word.
But then comes doubt, a quiet thief-
What if I burden them with grief?

What if there're busy, lost in thoughts?
What if my pain is overwrought?
What if their world holds heavier fears,
And mine feel small compared to theirs?

So I stay silent, wear a smile.
Pretend I'm fine, at least a while.
I build my walls, I brave the tide-
And hold the storm I feel inside.

10. The Silence She Taught Us.

She said,
"He's your Father-respect him."
Even when his words were knives,
and his silence, a storm.

She whispered,
"He's your brother-he means well."
As if bruises on our soul
were marks of familial love.

She insisted,
"He's elder-stay silent."
Because questioning was rebellion,
and obedience, our virtue.

But in the quiet of our thoughts,
We asked,
Why is our pain less important
than their pride?

Why does blood demand
our silence,
our submission,
our self?

We learned that love
doesn't demand bruises,
respect doesn't require fear,
and family shouldn't hurt.

So began to speak ,
to question,
to set boundaries
not as walls,
but as doors
to our own peace.

Now, teach ourselves:
Respect is mutual,
Love is gentle,
And silence is not always golden.

11. Suicides are stories left untold.

People often carry a notion-
That those who end their lives are weak.
But they don't see the silent battles,
The countless wars waged within,
Fought beneath smiles,
And behind tired eyes.

Time and again,
They stood at the edge,
Wrestling with thoughts
That whispered "unlive yourself."
The cruel echoes inside
That kept repeating,
"You won't make it trough."

And yet they rose-
Telling themselves
"It will be fine, just one more day..."
Until one day,

They could no longer fight back
The way they always used to.

So no,
They weren't weak.
They were warriors-
worn by the weight of unseen wars.

Suicides..
Are stories the world never paused to read.

12. Be Kind

Everyone is fighting a war,
An unsaid storm within-
Invisible to the world,
But fierce beneath the skin.

Each soul you meet is carrying.
A weight you cannot see.
Some bear it in their bodies,
Some in silent poverty.

Others smiles while breaking down,
Their mind a noisy maze,
Or hold back tears while standing tall
In life's relentless haze.

we're all on our own battlefield.
Wagging wars we didn't choose-
Against grief, against emptiness,
Against the fear to lose.

And though you may not understand
What someone's going through,
Your kindness might become the strength.
They never found in view.

Just staying - yes , just staying-
can be a quiet light.
A hand that holds, a heart that hears,
can help someone still fight.

So be the calm, the gentle breeze,
The peace they cannot find.
You never know the war you ease-
When you choose to be kind.

13. I am an Independent

I am an independent - strong and whole,
I don't need someone to complete my soul.
In the darkest night, I am my light,
A quiet flame that burns so bright.

At my lowest, I sit with pain,
Whispering, " You'll rise again."
I hold my heart when it feels tight,
And tell myself, " I'll be alright."

When storms rage loud, I stand my ground,
A warrior spirit, fierce and sound.
Through every trial, every fight,
I remind myself of my inner might.

Independent isn't just a coin or key,
It's the way I set my own spirit free.
Financially firm, emotionally clear-
I own my path, I steer, I steer.

I am an Independent- not by chance,
But through every fall, every stance,
I don't just survive .
I shine ,
I thrive.
Freely alive, freely alive.

14. The Power Within.

People and moments comes and go,
Like rivers in a steady flow.
They speak, they act, they try to sway,
But only you can light your way.

No word they say can make you fall,
Unless you choose to heed the call.
No storm can shake your rooted tree,
Unless you grant it liberty.

Their power fades, it's smoke and air,
Unless you meet it with a stare.
Your clam, your silence, your control-
That's the strength that makes you whole.

So hold peace, and let them be,
You're not a pawn, you hold the key.
For only when you bend or break.
Do they the reins of power take.

Stand tall, unshaken, wise and true-
People and things have no hold on you.

24

15. Finally, I know

Very late, but now I see-
I was never meant to search
For someone to complete me.
I only ever needed.
To be with myself.

We're born alone,
And we'll leave this world alone
So why not live
This one precious life
With our own heart
As our home?

Don't wait for love
To arrive in someone else's hands
Give it to yourself-
The way you always dreamed it.
Fully
Unapologetically.

This isn't about shutting others out,
But learning to stay in
When the world walks out.
Care for them,
But care for you, too.

You matter.
You always did,
And finally,
You know.

16. The Audacity of Hope.

We sleep each night
not knowing if morning will come,
yet still,
we plan-
a day,
a month,
a year ahead.

With heart full of unknowns,
we dare to dream,
mapping tomorrow
on fragile paper skies.

For though life is woven with
uncertainty,
we move forward-
quietly, bravely-
carrying hope
like a lantern in the dark.

17. To My Sister

I have you-
a quiet blessings,
a gift wrapped in laughter and chaos,
given to me by fate
through the hands of my parents.

In you, i found a sister-
not by blood,
but by something stronger,
A thread woven through soul and time.

You annoy me in ways
only someone who loves me could-
but even in your teasing,
I hear the hush of care
and feel the wrath of unspoken affection.

You're my living diary-
a keeper of my scattered thoughts,
my bottled emotions,

my unsaid words.
And I love you-
feel grateful to have you.

18. My brother, my shield

You are my armor, steadfast and true,
Enveloping me with protective embrace.
At times, your shield may press too close,
Yet within each bruise, your care I trace.

Harsh words like arrows, swiftly thrown,
Yet woven with the threads of love.
In sternness, seeds of strength are sown,
Guided by prayers sent above.

Unspoken, your love resonates deep,
In actions louder than words declare.
For your sisters, promises you keep,
A guardian always present there.

Through tempests fierce and shadows long,
Your presence is a beacon bright.
In silent gesture, love stands strong,
my brother, my protector, my light.

19. The Table Turns.

Time, it turns the table around,
Softly sweetly, without a sound.
There was a time when your mother dressed with grace,
Now you doll her up, a smile on her face.

You wore her *dupatta* as I *saree,* draped it with pride,
Pretending in play, with eyes open wide.
Now she watches with joy and glee,
As you twirl in her old sarees.

Our mother cooked our favorite dish with, love,
Now you serve hers, like a prayer above.
From tiny hands playing *ghar- ghar* all day,
To real talks of home in a grown-up way.

How gently the years rewrite the art-
Roles may shift, but never the heart.
In these circles, loves is fond...
As time keeps turning the table around.

20. Across Cities, Across Hearts.

Who knew the ones I once fought with,
Over toys, over space, over tiny little things,
Would one day be the ones I miss so deeply,
Their absence echoing louder than any shouting could
bring.

There was a time their laughter felt too loud,
Their teasing too much, their presence a crowd.
But time, that quiet magician, changed it all-
Now I crave those silly brawls.

The games we played have packed their bags,
The silly talks turned to deep midnight chats.
No more chasing victories on board games lands,
Now we share dreams held in trembling hands.

We live in different cities, we chase our own skies,
Yet somehow, in every hello and goodbye,
We find each other in memory, in heart in sign.

Sibling by chance,
Friend by choice,
Forever a part of each other's voice.

21. The Companion called struggle

Struggle is our truest friend-
born with us,
growing old beside us,
leaving only when we do.

it greets our first breath,
clings through every triumph,
whispers through each fall.

As infants, we reach
for meaning in the light,
crawl through confusion,
fall and rise again-
discovery dressed as difficulty.

in our teens, it shifts-
a shadow behind change.
Hormones flare,
heart flutter and crack,

exam weigh heavy,
friendship bend and break.
We stumble toward identity,
uncertain, but moving.

Adulthood brings,
a battlefield of choices-
college or career,
passion or practicality.
We chase placements,
forge memories,
taste our first heartbreak.
Some seek to make their parents proud,
others seek a self still unknown.

Then comes the race-
not one we chose,
but one we run.
Deadlines, Appraisals.
Graveyard shifts for distant dreams.
Choosing love, building homes,
balancing dreams with duty-
struggle become our routine.

In middle age,
we turn to our children.
We give what we never had,

carry their futures on tired backs,
sacrificing quietly
for smiles we may never fully understand.

And when they've grown and flown,
our bodies begin their silent rebellion-
aching knees, brittle bones,
a slow, steady reminder:
even time struggle to hold us.

Struggle is fair,
if nothing else.
The rich wrestle with keeping it all,
the poor with having enough.
Different forms, same fire.

It is not our foe-
struggle teaches.
It sculpts strength,
breeds empathy,
reveal the depth of our courage.

To walk with it is not to be broken,
but to become whole.